A Naturalist's Guide to the Southern Palisades

NMS PO Box 720, Palisades, New York 10964-0720

Library of Congress Control Number: 2006900203
Slowik, Nancy
 A Naturalist's Guide to the Southern Palisades
ISBN 0-9769428-0-1

Credits and Acknowledgements

Cover and interior photographs: Sandra Guasti Bonardi

Art director and designer: Janet Slowik

Illustration of maps: Ray Cruz

Fonts: Elegante and Frutiger

Printer: Phoenix Color Corporation

Printed in New Jersey

A Note from the Author

This field guide represents the combined efforts of several very talented people. The entire project was designed and produced by art director and sister, Janet Slowik. Her creative layout and attention to detail produced an attractive, easy to use field guide. Sandra Bonardi photographed all the images contained in this book. Graphic artist Ray Cruz created all of the trail maps that were drawn to correspond with each walk. I am extremely grateful to this team of artists for all their work.

Many thanks to Jim Hall of the Palisades Interstate Park for permission to create this field guide. As the naturalist-director of Greenbrook Sanctuary, my unique relationship with the park has given me the opportunity to explore the southern Palisades in all seasons. Finally, I would like to thank my husband, Tim Brandon, for proof reading the script and offering words of encouragement throughout the project.

NMS PO Box 720, Palisades, New York 10964   ISBN 0-976-9428-0-1

INTRODUCTION ❧

T he southern portion of the Palisades Interstate Park is best known for its breathtaking vistas and unique geology. Once primarily a recreational park, steep vertical ascents continue to challenge avid hikers. For those who prefer a more leisurely stroll, several trails offer an easier approach. Throughout the park's long history, visitors have always enjoyed the opportunity to observe nature, in such close proximity to a metropolitan area. This field guide is designed to continue that tradition, encouraging an appreciation of the park's wilder side for both beginning and experienced nature enthusiasts.

The southern portion of the park is barely visible on a map, and may account for why it remains a wild area. The rugged topography of the Palisades on the west, and the Hudson River bordering on the east provides a linear buffer zone. By limiting human access these natural features have served to protect the local plants and wildlife.

This area is considered an ecotone – a contact zone where several habitats merge. At the base of the cliff visitors can walk along the river, a riparian habitat that is part of the Hudson River tidal estuary. Nearby is the boulder habitat known as a talus slope. Classified in the Natural Heritage database of New Jersey as rare, this habitat harbors several endangered species. Well above the river, and along the top of the Palisades, you can explore the rocky cliff edge. Many unusual native plants and animals have adapted to life in this extremely dry and rugged location. Inland a mixed-oak woodland predominates, a habitat typical of northern New Jersey forests. Finally, several streams flow toward and empty into the Hudson River, creating a number of wooded wetlands.

Although fragmented by the parkway, the linear nature of the park provides local wildlife with an important and largely connected corridor along the Hudson River. In such a densely populated and developed area, this parkland has become even more precious to resident, migratory, and breeding wildlife populations. The continued development of farms, woodlands and wetlands has diminished the remaining populations of flora and fauna, leaving the Palisades as their last sanctuary.

The Palisades Interstate Park system is uniquely governed by two states, New York and New Jersey. Enormous in size, it encompasses more than 100,000 acres of parkland and historic sites. The New Jersey section is primarily a thin parcel of land that parallels the Hudson River for approximately 12 miles. The magnificent diabase cliffs rise dramatically near the shore of the river, to heights of 530 feet at Point Lookout. In 1983, the Palisades was designated a National Natural Landmark, considered the best example of a thick diabase sill in the United States. As you hike north and step across the state border into New York, it is evident why an interstate partnership was the only way to preserve the uninterrupted beauty that defines the park. As you continue north, the views of the river from Tallman Mountain State Park allow you to see one of the best examples of a salt marsh estuary preserved along the lower Hudson River.

After leading hikes for more than a decade in this area, I have selected a few of my favorite nature walks. My selection was based on consistently finding wildlife and interesting plants in varied habitats. Each hike is described verbally and ranked with the degree of difficulty and approximate length of the walk. Seasonal nature sightings are listed, but each hiker will have their own unique experience. Some of these hikes are remote and difficult. It is best to wear hiking boots, travel with a companion, and carry a cell phone if possible. Hikes are enhanced if you bring a pair of binoculars. We hope by using this field guide on your next walk along the Palisades, you will be able to observe and appreciate some of our natural treasures in the park.

What to Bring on Your Hike

Binoculars

Hand lens for plant identification

Additional field guides

Notebook and pencil

Water

Snack or lunch

Cell phone

Hiking companion if possible

Small first aid kit

Map of area

Rain gear

It's always a good idea to let someone know where you will be and when you plan to return.

Park Rules

The park is open from dawn to dusk.

Seasonal parking fees charged and senior citizen passes are available at Park Headquarters.

Please observe rules posted at each site as some vary slightly.

Bicycles are permitted on roads only, NOT on trails.

Dogs are permitted in some locations and only on a six foot leash.

DO NOT remove plants or animals from the park.

The park is patrolled by Parkway Police.
Please report inappropriate behavior to park staff.

NJ Parkway Police: 201-768-6001

TABLE OF CONTENTS

Hike 1
Undercliff Trail

**Linear Trail
~ 1-1/4 miles
round trip**

**Circular Loop
~ 2 miles**

Easy to moderate

**Park in Englewood
Boat Basin**

Easy hiking with a few moderate, rocky sections. There is a short climb if you choose one of the two high tide alternative trails. Try to time your walk at low tide.

Habitats— Riparian, and talus slope.

Interesting plants— Dutchman's pipe, black walnut tree, groundsel tree, false indigo, wild pink, red-berried elder, bladdernut, salt marsh cord grass, Mexican tea, seaside goldenrod, five-leaved akebia vine.

Interesting animals— Pipevine swallowtail butterfly, orchard oriole, great horned owl, red-breasted nuthatch, winter wren, American redstart, yellow warbler, hairy woodpecker, canvasback duck.

Unique natural feature— The presence of salt marsh plants and the close proximity of the trail to the Hudson River suggests a day at the beach.

Trail Description

This hike offers a relatively easy walking trail along the Hudson River. Begin your walk at the large, stone ruin that faces a sandy, tidal beach. As you walk north along the Shore Trail (white blaze) note the depth of the tide along the rock wall. If you have timed your hike at high tide the lower trail may be flooded and you will be forced to follow the alternate pathway marked High Tide Trail. The Hudson River is a tidal estuary where one can enjoy the smell of salt water and listen to the lapping waves as the tide rises and falls. The southern portion of the Hudson River contains higher concentrations of salt, which decrease in salinity as you travel north. The salty nature of this section of the river is reflected in the vegetation and animals found along the sea wall. When the tide is low, hikers can observe aquatic plants such as bulbous rockweed covering the rocks. In the intertidal zone you can also find the discarded shells of blue crabs, since this part of the river serves as a nursery for this species. A few remaining patches of salt marsh cord grass (Spartina alterniflora) still grow along portions of the sea wall, a reminder of the more extensive salt marsh that once thrived along the banks of this river.

Intertidal zone with rockweed.

As you continue walking north, look for distinctive plants such as red-berried elder, Mexican tea (an aromatic herb) and seaside goldenrod. Weathered pieces of sandstone, can frequently be found in colorful red and purple fragments along the trail. As you travel north, you will soon arrive at a second sandy beach area, a good place to look for tracks and animal sign in the sand. Continue north on the trail to the second stone ruin that once served as a park bathhouse. Stop and spend a little time in the open, grassy area. In spring it's a good place to observe migrating birds. In spring and summer you can observe local butterflies such as pipevine and tiger swallowtails as well as breeding birds such as the orchard oriole and yellow warbler. In winter the river harbors over-wintering ducks such as canvasback, common golden-eye and common merganser. Mixed flocks of white-throated sparrow,

Undercliff bathhouse.

dark-eyed junco, black-capped chickadee, and downy woodpecker find food and shelter along the Hudson River shoreline, critical to their survival in winter.

Just north of the second bathhouse is a cobblestone path that leads up to the Lower Road. Follow the path to the road which is also known as the Henry Hudson Drive, which will connect you to the Undercliff Picnic area. Watch for cars and bikes as you cross the drive. If you packed your lunch or brought a snack this is the best place to stop for a break. Undercliff, a remote area that is usually closed to cars, is only open to parking during the height of the busy season. Used exclusively for special events, it is frequented by hikers, bikers, and of course, wildlife. In late spring and early summer it's a good area to observe many of the birds that breed along the Palisades. American redstart, rose-breasted grosbeak, Baltimore oriole, eastern towhee, Carolina and winter wren, wild turkey, eastern phoebe, veery and great horned owl have all

Picnic area at Undercliff.

been recorded as breeding birds in this area. In winter it is a good place to search for red-breasted nuthatches, ruby-crowned kinglets, winter wrens and hairy woodpeckers. You may even hear the calls of the resident great horned owl that frequent this area. Several black walnut trees grow in the center of Undercliff next to towering tulip trees. An invasive, horticultural vine known as five-leaved akebia can be found covering some of these trees. White pine trees can also be found here and are a good place to search for birds, particularly in winter. West of the picnic area is a talus slope, a unique and endangered habitat in New Jersey. Large boulders continue to separate and fall from the upper cliff face. These rock piles are home to unique plants and animals that have adapted to this constantly changing habitat. Just south of the picnic area is a small cemetery that has extensive stands of bladdernut, a native shrub with a distinctive bladder-shaped seed pod. Usually you can find a number of resident northern cardinals here in any season.

You have the option to return on the Henry Hudson Drive ONLY if the road is closed to traffic. If the road is open to cars at the time you are hiking, you should return on the Shore Trail, since there is no designated walking path on the road. (Note: the road is usually closed to automobiles from November to late April, depending on weather conditions.) To return to the shore trail, enter from the road just south of Undercliff picnic area, near the second sandy beach.

The preferred route to return is via the Henry Hudson Drive. As you walk south along the road in late spring and summer, look for the large, heart-shaped leaves of Dutchman's pipe, the host plant for the locally abundant pipevine swallowtail butterfly. This vine grows to great heights by winding around trees and was once planted as a vertical screen by estate gardeners. A native of the Appalachian Mountain woodlands, it now thrives in the southern section of the New Jersey Palisades. Also watch for the iridescent blue of the pipevine swallowtail butterfly associated

Wild pinks growing on the cliffs.

Dutchman's Pipe.

with this plant. It can be seen at all stages of its life cycle here.

As you descend the roadway to the boat basin and parking area, remember to search the cliff face for wildflowers. In early to mid-May, the brightly colored wild pink can be found growing from the crevices of the rock face where the Henry Hudson Drive intersects with the road known as Dyckman Hill and connects to the boat basin below. Follow the road to the end of the stone wall, and make a left at the staircase. The parking lot is north of the picnic area.

**Parking Area–Northern lot in Englewood Boat Basin (seasonal parking fees).
Senior citizen passes are available at the Park Headquarters.**

Pipevine Swallowtail Butterfly.

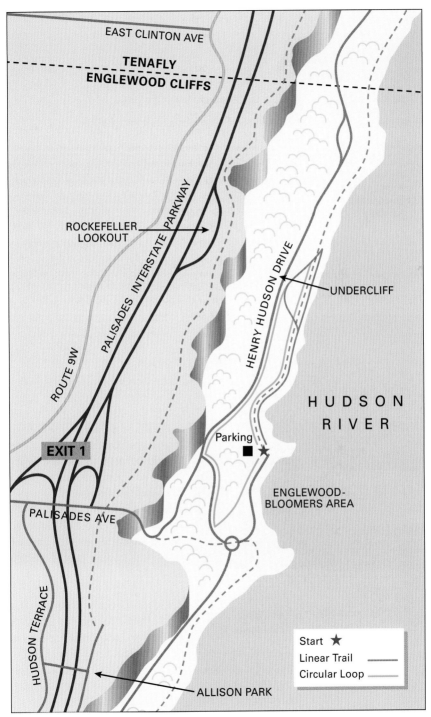

EAST CLINTON AVE

TENAFLY
ENGLEWOOD CLIFFS

ROCKEFELLER
LOOKOUT

PALISADES INTERSTATE PARKWAY

ROUTE 9W

HENRY HUDSON DRIVE

UNDERCLIFF

HUDSON
RIVER

Parking

EXIT 1

ENGLEWOOD-
BLOOMERS AREA

PALISADES AVE

HUDSON TERRACE

ALLISON PARK

Start ★
Linear Trail
Circular Loop

Map of Hike 1 – Undercliff Trail

Hike 2
Alpine Long Path

**Linear Trail
~ 1-1/2 mile
round trip**

Easy

**Limited parking
at the Park
Headquarters,
Exit 2 from
Parkway**

Easiest and shortest hike in the guide.

Habitats—Cliff edge, mixed oak woodland.

Interesting plants—There are many non-native, horticultural plants that have survived the former estates. These exotics can be found growing among native trees and shrubs.

Interesting animals—Chipping sparrow, cedar waxwing, migrant and resident raptors along vistas such as red-tailed hawk, turkey vulture and peregrine falcon.

Unique natural feature—The natural crevice known as Gray Crag, that separates the Palisades rock is of particular interest.

Trail Description

This is the easiest and most accessible of all the hikes listed in the guide. You will be hiking on the Long Path (aqua blaze), which travels along the top of the Palisades and near the Palisades Interstate Parkway. The Park Headquarters is found in one of the few remaining estates that once dotted the cliffs. Today it houses the New Jersey Park Headquarters and the Parkway Police, offering visitor information, rest rooms and a water fountain.

Park headquarters at Alpine, NJ.

Begin your hike from the north end of the parking lot. Eastern red cedars border the parking area and are a good place to search for cedar waxwings. In spring and summer listen and look for indigo buntings, northern mockingbirds, and chipping sparrows that breed in this area. As you enter the trail you will find a few structural remnants of former estates. Many introduced plant species have persisted long after the estate houses were removed and offer additional evidence of their original grandeur. Examples of these plants include Norway spruce, Norway maple, winged euonymous, Japanese red maple, wineberry, periwinkle, English ivy and spring bulbs such as snowdrops and grape muscaria. Native trees such as wild black cherry, sassafras, white oak, red oak, sugar and red maple grow alongside these non-native plants.

The most obvious, and persistent aspect of this trail is the traffic noise from the Palisades Interstate Parkway. Originally envisioned as a scenic roadway bringing visitors to the Park, today the Parkway is instead largely utilized by commuters. Creative interpreters have suggested you drown out the noise by imaging it as the sound of the ocean. This can be difficult in portions of the trail where you are extremely close to the road.

After walking for approximately three-quarters of a mile, watch for an obvious divide in the Palisades ridge. You can see where the diabase rock has separated, creating a deep ravine. At this point, follow the ravine until you see a man-made cement bridge. You have reached the area known as Gray Crag. After you

Foot bridge at Gray Crag.

cross the bridge you can see an excellent example of the rock columns or pillars, which were once common along the Palisades before quarrying began. In early fall watch for broad-winged hawks, osprey and other migrating raptors. In winter, bald eagles can be observed from this vista. Take care not to touch the poison ivy that grows abundantly in this area. Staghorn sumac and ailanthus trees are the most common woody plants here.

Continuing north on the Long Path, you will find several small streams that intersect this trail, and in early spring this area can be quite wet. Plan to wear appropriate footwear. In some spots rocks and boards have been placed to assist you on your walk. By late summer most of this area will be quite dry, including these intermittent streams. A footbridge signals that you have reached one of the wider and more permanent streams. Just south of the stream and bridge, locate a small pathway to the cliff edge. Here you will find a sheer cliff with a dramatic waterfall, depending upon the rainfall amounts and the season. As you look north watch for resident red-tailed hawks or turkey vultures. During fall migration, twelve species of different raptors can be observed from this vista. Please take care in this fragile area. Many plants that cannot grow in the woodland, inhabit these cliff edge sites. Hillside blueberry, staghorn sumac, and hackberry are just a few of the woody plants that grow here. A stand of partridgeberry, a low growing evergreen wildflower, grows in the crevices of the diabase rock alongside haircap moss. Lichens, a unique combination

Falls near Gray Crag.

of blue-green algae and fungi, stain the rocks that frame the waterfall. This is a great place to pause and listen, as the fresh water from above joins the brackish water below.

Since this is a linear trail, you must return along the same path. I am always amazed at the different plants and animals I see hiking the same trail in a different direction. This is a good opportunity for you to do the same.

Park your car in the northern section of the Alpine Headquarters parking lot. There is no fee, but you should limit your parking time. Keep in mind that Tuesday afternoon traffic court is in session, and parking is very limited.

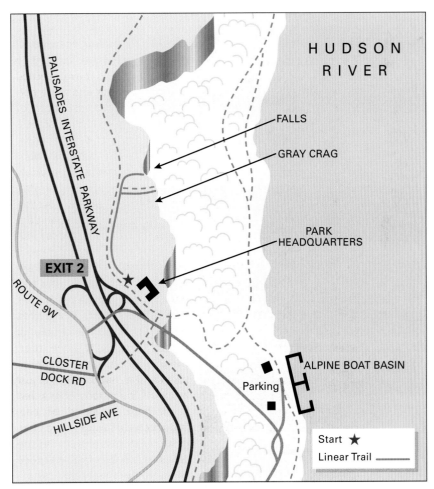

Map of Hike 2 – Alpine Long Path

Hike 3
Alpine Shore Trail

Circular Loop
~ 2-3/4 miles

Easy to moderate

**Park in Alpine
Boat Basin –
Seasonal fees**

Easy overall trail conditions, moderate along the lower portion of the shore trail.

Habitats—Riparian, mixed oak woodland, talus slope.

Interesting plants—Early spring wildflowers include wild ginger, early meadow rue, yellow forest violet, Dutchman's breeches, spring beauty, wild geranium.

Interesting animals—The best trail to find breeding birds such as worm-eating warbler, scarlet tanager, and wood thrush. Black rat snakes can be common.

Unique feature—This well marked portion of the trail offers many of the best opportunities to see wildlife in the southern Palisades. A wide variety of plants typical of the New Jersey Palisades can also be found growing in this habitat. It is my favorite of all the nature hikes listed in this field guide, and I lead a hike on this trail at least once a year. In spring the trail offers the best variety of spring wildflowers, migrating warblers, interesting breeding birds and the occasional reptile. The fall season promises good views of osprey fishing on the Hudson and monarch butterflies feeding on seaside goldenrod. In winter, you can view over-wintering waterfowl such as canvasback, common goldeneye and common merganser ducks at closer range than from above on the cliff edge. Interesting wildlife can be observed year round.

Trail Description

Begin your walk at the historic Kearney House. Directly behind the house and along the stream, you can find purple sandstone crumbling faster than the gray diabase. In late spring and early summer the picnic area is a good place to watch for breeding barn swallows as they whiz past you at high speeds. They nest along the pier and on the boathouse. Baltimore oriole, eastern kingbird, and warbling vireo can also be found nesting in the London plane trees that grow in the parking area.

The Kearney House at Alpine Boat Basin.

Start your ascent at the base of the old cobble stone road just north of the Kearney House on the Shore Trail (white blaze). Although the trail usually travels alongside the Hudson River, this section rises above. As you travel along the trail you will find several freshwater streams. In early spring this section of the trail is a good area to find migrating warblers and other passerine birds as they rest and refuel for their trip north. Some migrant species will stay here to breed on the rocky, wooded slope. This habitat attracts ground-nesting birds such as worm-eating warbler, and black and white warbler. Scarlet tanager, wood thrush, Louisiana waterthrush and red-eyed vireo are also regular breeders here.

As you travel north you will come upon an opening where non-native plants predominate. This open area

The Alpine Pavilion.

Historic marker denotes the beginning of hike.

is a good place to look for butterflies in the summer and ruby-throated hummingbirds in the fall. Day lilies, wisteria, and Japanese honeysuckle are part of a vine community that attracts breeding gray catbird, northern cardinal, and the secretive brown thrasher.

Continue north and you will come to a fork in the trail marked by two white arrows. The trail on the right (lower road) will take you north along the river on a rocky footpath. The trail on the left will continue to follow the upper road, well above the river on an earthen footpath. Since the two trails will intersect approximately one mile north, you can choose either trail. I prefer to travel north on the upland trail and return south on the lowland trail. The connecting trail, known as a switchback, is much easier to locate from the upper trail. Here it simply descends and connects with the lower trail at the river. If you are traveling north on the lower trail you will have to carefully watch for this switchback as you follow the Hudson River. The upland fork of the Shore Trail offers inter-

Intermittent stream along Shore Trail.

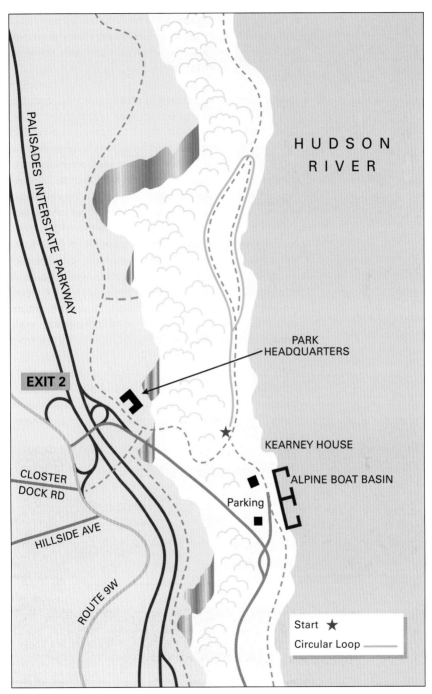

Map of Hike 3 – Alpine Shore Trail

HUDSON RIVER

PALISADES INTERSTATE PARKWAY

EXIT 2

PARK HEADQUARTERS

KEARNEY HOUSE

CLOSTER DOCK RD

ALPINE BOAT BASIN

Parking

HILLSIDE AVE

ROUTE 9W

Start ★

Circular Loop

esting early spring wildflowers and ferns. The lowland fork provides salt spray breezes and closer views of the river. Take note that the lower trail has its share of poison ivy in summer.

Spring wildflowers highlight the upper trail and can be found blooming from late April into May. Dutchman's breeches are more commonly seen along the rocky hillsides while spring beauty is restricted to areas along the path. Both are early bloomers and relatively common in areas. Wildflowers such as Jack-in-the-pulpit, wild geranium, hairy and false Solomon seal, common blue violet, Herb Robert and wild sarsaparilla can also be found sporadically along this trail. Yellow forest violet, perfoliate bellwort, wild ginger, and early meadow rue also grow here, but are less common and occur in smaller numbers. Christmas and New York fern can also be found growing in and around the wildflowers. Competition with invading non-native plants continues to displace these wild natives at an alarming rate.

The black rat snake can be observed at any point along this trail and occasionally can be seen climbing trees as it hunts for nestling birds. The copperhead snake is much rarer and is usually found along the rocky portion of the trail near the river.

The entire loop takes about 2–3 hours to complete, depending upon your speed and degree of nature watching.

Hike 4
Forest View Trail

Two choices:

Trail A

A linear hike, shorter in length but with more difficult hiking conditions. Hikers must descend and ascend the Palisades along a steep and rugged trail.

Habitats—Mixed oak woodland, cliff edge, riparian, old field-meadow, and talus slope.

Interesting plants—Perfoliate bellwort, pale jewelweed, red-berried elder, alternate-leaved dogwood.

Interesting animals—Northern copperhead and black rat snake are uncommon, Carolina wren, black and white and worm-eating warbler along the ridge trail, and yellow warbler, ruby-throated hummingbird and common yellow-throat warbler nest in more open areas of the field below.

Unique natural feature—This is a wild and rugged trail representative of all the habitats found in the southern Palisades.

Trail B

A linear three mile hike traveling in one direction, requiring two cars and at least two hikers to participate, and return by car.

Difficult hiking conditions descending the Palisades, easy to moderate hiking conditions along the shore trail.

Habitats—Mixed oak woodland, cliff edge, riparian, talus slope.

Interesting Plants—All the plants observed in Hike A as well as paper birch, Appalachian gooseberry, round-leaved dogwood, rock cap polypody fern and wild sarsaparilla.

Interesting Animals—Many of the same animals listed in Hike A with opportunities to view red-tailed hawks and turkey vulture soaring along the cliff.

Linear Trail with two choices

Trail A ~ 1-3/4 mile round trip

Trail B ~ 3-1/4 miles one way

Both hikes are difficult

Park along Route 9W (east side) just south of Camp Alpine Greater New York Councils

This is the most challenging hike in this guide with two alternative hikes to choose from.

Note: Trail β will require some pre-planning and a partner.

Trail Description

Trail A. Linear Forest View Hike North (descent and ascent).

This hike is shorter but more difficult. You should be in good physical condition before attempting this trail. Hiking boots are strongly recommended.

Begin by crossing the footbridge over the Palisades Interstate Parkway. After exiting the bridge, look for the blue and white blaze of the Forest View Trail. As you travel east toward the cliff you can see a variety of trees and shrubs that are characteristic of a northern mixed-oak community. Several species of oak and hickory predominate, with an understory of shadbush and maple-leaf viburnum. On your right (south) there is an open field where you can stop to look and listen for nesting blue-winged warblers, and indigo buntings in late spring. As you continue east you will intersect the Long Path (aqua blaze). Shortly after you

Foot path across Palisades Interstate Parkway from Route 9W.

pass the Long Path you will see a stone building known as the Women's Federation Monument. Built in the 1929, it pays tribute to the pioneering efforts of the women that helped preserve the Palisades.

There are several interesting plants that surround this open area. Just west of the monument is a stand of arrow-leaved violet, and the rare one-flowered cancer-root. Closer to the cliff you should be able to find wild pink in spring. This plant is rare in New Jersey, but locally uncommon on the NJ Palisades. To the south there is an open field that supports sweet-scented Joe-pye-weed and several species of goldenrod. Along the cliff edge you can find hackberry trees dwarfed in size by their sterile growing conditions, and low growing shrubs such as hillside blueberry and black huckleberry.

Women's Federation Monument.

The vista alongside the Women's Federation Monument offers dramatic views of the Hudson River. Depending on the tide, you should be able to see portions of a former pier. Double-crested cormorants often perch here as they dry their wings. In the fall you may see some of the hawk migration from this vantage point, although there is a better view at Point Lookout just north of this site. The trail travels north briefly, then you descend the Palisades along a series of steep stairs. Watch your footing.

Pier at Forest View.

This is a wonderful trail for early spring wildflowers. Highlights include early saxifrage, wild columbine, hairy Solomon's seal, wild geranium, perfoliate bellwort and Jack-in-the-pulpit. Ferns such as marginal wood fern, and Christmas fern grow along the steep embankments. As you descend, note the changes in vegetation. Near the bottom of the climb you can find pale jewelweed and red-berried elder growing on the rocky talus slope. This is also a good place to find worm-eating and black and white warblers on breeding territory in spring and summer. Also watch for giant millipedes along this trail, a larger version of the more familiar "thousand-legged" invertebrate that can be found in your garden.

At the bottom of the trail turn left and walk north following the Shore Trail (white blaze) until you reach an open field-meadow. There are many non-native plants growing in this open area including the invasive porcelain-berry and purple loosestrife. Growing near these aggressive plants are some native species such as common milkweed, Joe-pye-weed and several species of goldenrods. This is a very good place to see local butterflies in the summer such as tiger swallowtail, hackberry, spicebush swallowtail, mourning cloak, and monarch. Ruby-throated hummingbirds have been recorded breeding in this area as well as yellow warblers and common yellowthroat. Walk north to the stream and listen for the loud song of the Carolina wren. The relative inaccessibility of this area helps to maintain its wild character.

Return the same way you descended. You will be surprised at all the plants you missed on the way down. Drink plenty of water and climb slowly as this is a steep ascent.

Trail Description

Trail B. Linear Forest View Hike South (two cars).

You must be hiking with at least two people. Leave one car at the north end of the Alpine Boat Basin (seasonal fees), and the other parked along Route 9W by the footbridge at the start of the trail.

This is a long hike that begins the same as the Forest View hike A. When you get to the bottom of the Palisades you will make a right turn, heading south on the Shore Trail (follow the white blaze). Along the trail there are impenetrable thickets of multiflora rose, Asiatic bittersweet and Japanese honeysuckle, which provide cover for nesting birds such as gray catbird, northern cardinal and American robin. These tend to grow primarily along the eastern side of the trail. As you continue to walk south, notice the change in vegetation on the west side of the trail. Here you are walking along the edge of the talus slope, classified by the state as an endangered habitat in New Jersey. Noticeably cooler temperatures in summer enable plants that usually occur in more northern regions to grow in this area. As a result, the talus slope is home to several rare plants and animals that in some instances are found in few other places in New Jersey. This habitat is subject to constant change as new boulders fall away from the upper cliffs. Use caution in late winter and early spring.

Stands of paper birch, Appalachian gooseberry, round-leaved dogwood, rock cap polpody and wild sarsaparilla are common in this area. Plants that have escaped cultivation during the days of estate gardens such as deutzia, can be found growing here.

View of cliffs from Shore Trail south of Forest View.

Salt marsh cordgrass along the Hudson River.

Continue hiking south along the Shore Trail remembering to look up at the majestic cliffs above. From this vantage point you can observe eastern red cedars growing from the cliff face, a tree that was once more common along the cliff edge. Be sure to note the plants that grow along the riverbank of the Shore Trail. Beach plants such as seaside goldenrod, salt marsh cord grass and spearscale are reminders that the Hudson is governed by the tides and is brackish in nature. Stands of bitter dock border the trails as you move southward.

As you continue south along the shore trail, at mile 1.85 you will reach a switchback where you can opt to take the upper or lower shore trail. Either one will bring you back to the Alpine Boat Basin. See Hike 3 for a description of this portion of the walk.

Park one car in the Alpine Boat Basin and the second along Route 9W on the east side of the road just south of The Boy Scout Camp, the Greater New York Council. Note the parking hours and restrictions along Route 9W.

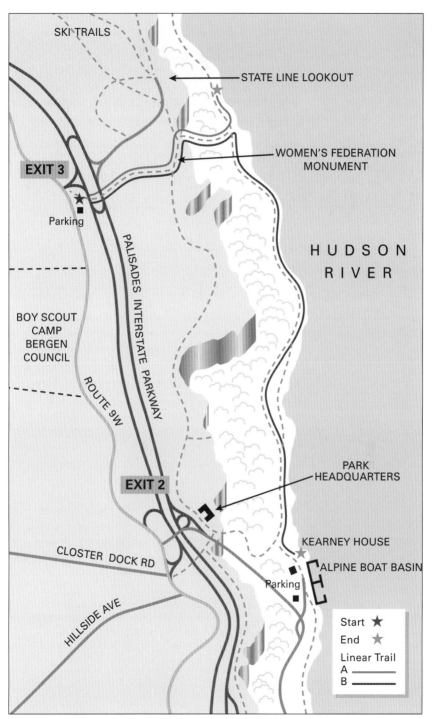

SKI TRAILS

STATE LINE LOOKOUT

WOMEN'S FEDERATION
MONUMENT

EXIT 3

Parking

PALISADES INTERSTATE PARKWAY

BOY SCOUT
CAMP
BERGEN
COUNCIL

ROUTE 9W

H U D S O N
R I V E R

PARK
HEADQUARTERS

EXIT 2

KEARNEY HOUSE

CLOSTER DOCK RD

ALPINE BOAT BASIN

Parking

HILLSIDE AVE

Start ★
End ★
Linear Trail
A ———
B ———

Map of Hike 4 – Forest View Trail

Hike 5
Tallman Trail

**Circular Loop
~ 2-3/4 miles**

Easy

**Park in lot off
Route 9W in
Palisades, NY**

This trail is relatively flat and easy to walk. Insect spray is strongly recommended in late spring and summer.

Habitats—Woodland swamp, mixed oak woodland, cliff edge, salt marsh.

Interesting plants—Dutchman's breeches, spring beauty, round-leaved pyrola, round-leaved hepatica.

Interesting animals—Many amphibians breed in this wetland area, including wood frog, spring peeper, gray tree frog, and spotted salamander. Resident screech owl, great horned owl and wood duck can also be found here. Northern harrier, great blue heron, and great egret can be spotted in the salt marsh.

Unique features—The overhead view of an extensive salt marsh along the Hudson River is breathtaking. The wetland pools were created for a tank farm in 1928, and are now a critical breeding area for many species of amphibians.

*Parking area for Tallman
State Park from Route 9W.*

View of Piermont Marsh.

Trail Description

Begin the hike from the parking area by following the bike path and the Long Path as they travel together in an easterly direction. This is also a favorite jogging and dog walking trail. After 1/4 mile, the Long Path will turn north (left), and continue through an extensive wooded wetland. You may choose to follow this alternate route (see map). The extensive wetland on the left is a good area to observe migrating warblers in spring and fall in addition to wood ducks and screech owl which breed here. If you continue along the bike path, at approximately 1/2 mile, watch carefully for the trail marker on the right. Turn right, and travel along this narrow trail.

This portion of the hiking trail is not blazed, and parallels the Hudson River. When you reach the vista, take time to enjoy the view. You are overlooking Piermont Marsh, one of the largest remaining salt marshes in the area. It is federally protected as part of the Hudson River National Estuarine Research Reserve, and managed by New York State Department of Environmental Conservation, DEC.

From this vantage point, you can distinguish one of the three unique vegetation zones that comprise the salt marsh. This area is known as the tidal wetland, and located near or above mean high tide. It harbors a variety of plants and animals all regulated by their proximity to the river. Growing along the edge of the river, is salt marsh cord grass, *Spartina alterniflora*, one of the most important species to provide food and habitat for fish, crustaceans and birds. Further inland is the low growing mat known as the salt meadow. It was once predominately comprised of salt hay, *Spartina patens*, and grows in combination with spike grass, three-square rush and common reed. This area serves as a critical buffer zone between the land and river, filtering sediments and providing food for upland birds and mammals. Watch for northern harriers, once known as the marsh hawk as they comb the area. Great blue heron, great egret, and several species of ducks can be found along the meandering waterways in the marsh. Red fox, muskrat, marsh wren, least bittern and Virginia rail, have all been recorded here.

What cannot be seen from this vantage point are the other two vegetation zones, and the wildlife it supports. In and around the tidal shallows, and mudflats live fiddler crab, marsh snail, diamondback terrapin turtle and numerous species of fish. These are best viewed by paddling in a canoe.

Route 9W Golf – North of Tallman parking lot.

Shadbush and flowering dogwood surround this vista as well as staghorn sumac, which grows closer to the cliff edge. All three species provide edible berries for migrating and resident birds. As you return to the trail you will find a wetland woods whose tree species include sweet gum, black sour gum, and swamp white oak. In early spring, the tiny yellow flowers of spicebush dominate the understory. Later in the season

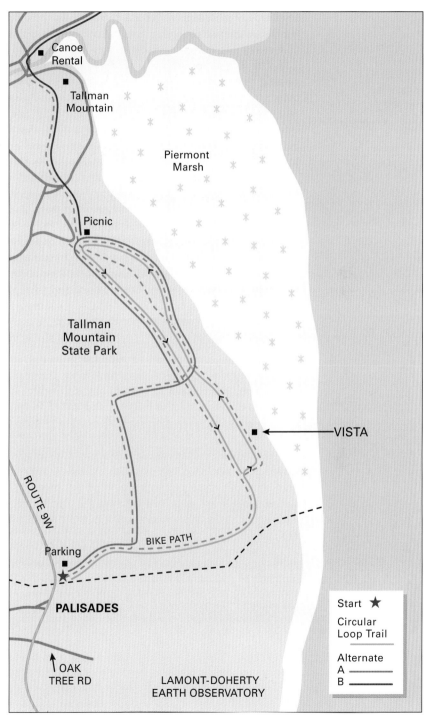

Canoe
Rental

Tallman
Mountain

Piermont
Marsh

Picnic

Tallman
Mountain
State Park

VISTA

ROUTE 9W

BIKE PATH

Parking

PALISADES

OAK
TREE RD

LAMONT-DOHERTY
EARTH OBSERVATORY

Start ★

Circular
Loop Trail

Alternate
A ————
B ————

Map of Hike 5 – Tallman Trail

shrubs like highbush blueberry and black haw provide fruit for wildlife.

This trail is well known for a spectacular wildflower display in the spring. Hillsides of Dutchman's breeches bloom in late April. Skunk cabbage blooms as early as February and by April the cabbage-like leaves fill the wetland areas. Spring beauty, wild geranium, hairy Solomon's seal and false Solomon's seal also bloom in this area. Less common along this path is the round-leaved pyrola and hepatica. Many migrating warblers can be found in this area during spring and fall and it is a particularly good site to find palm warblers, an early spring migrant. As you travel north you will come to picnic tables and rest rooms at 1-1/2 miles, a good place to take a break and have lunch or a snack. I like to return on the bike path, which creates a nice loop and is an easy walk back to the parking lot.

There are two alternative routes to this hike.

A. Follow the Long Path for the entire walk to view the woodland vernal ponds, which were excavated in 1928, by Standard Oil for use as a tank farm, and then abandoned. If you take this route you will miss the first vista overlooking the marsh as described in the original walk.

B. Follow the Long Path down to Piermont Marsh and walk out to the pier. This significantly longer hike is well worth the time, but you should plan accordingly. Canoe rentals are available at Paradise Boats, Inc., located at 15 Paradise Avenue, Piermont, NY 10968 845-359-0073

The parking lot is located on the east side of Route 9W, just north of the Oak Tree Road traffic light.
Landmarks to help find the parking lot include a vintage gas station to the south, and a golf range to the north.
Parking space is limited since there is no parking fee.

ADDITIONAL SITES TO VISIT IN THE PARK

Henry Hudson Drive

This is a very scenic drive that travels along the bottom of the Palisades. You can observe the Hudson River and a portion of Greenbrook Falls along this road. Note that the road is closed during winter months. Take the Palisades Interstate Parkway to Exit 2. Go past the park headquarters, traveling down the Alpine Approach Road. Drive south along the Henry Hudson Drive to Dyckman Hill Road, just above Englewood Boat Basin. Bear right on this road back to Exit 1 on the Palisades Interstate Parkway.

Greenbrook Sanctuary

This 165 acre nature preserve is open year round to members. Palisades Nature Association administers a variety of nature programs in the park and the surrounding Palisades. Group visits are by appointment and a visitor's day opens the sanctuary to the public. Access to the park is off Route 9W, approximately .8 miles north of Clinton Avenue, Tenafly, N.J. Call 201-768-1360 for membership.

State Line Lookout

This popular site features Point Lookout, the highest vista in the New Jersey section of the Palisades. A restaurant, gift shop and bathrooms are available at the lookout. Ski trails for cross country skiing are a popular winter attraction. A self-guided nature trail is available. Access from the Palisades Interstate Parkway between Exit 2 and 3.

PLANTS OF THE PALISADES ❧

A wide diversity of habitats combined with a unique geology has created an interesting local flora in the Southern Palisades. This plant listing represents a small sample of species either commonly found here or considered rare in the area. Some of these plants escaped cultivation from estate gardens that existed prior to the formation of the Palisades Interstate Park.

Unfortunately several alien species continue to invade significant portions of the park, overwhelming both native and naturalized species. Despite this trend, many native plants can still be found within the park.

A more complete plant inventory is available from the staff at Greenbrook Sanctuary.

*Asterisk denotes plant is non-native species.

Spicebush, *Lindera benzoin*
Laurel Family

This shrub can be found growing in the under-story of moist woodlands. The tiny yellow flowers are among the first to bloom in early April, but the fruits do not ripen until September, providing an important food for migrating birds. All parts of the plant produce an aromatic fragrance when crushed.

Forsythia*, *Forsythia x intermedia*
Olive Family

A native of Eurasia, this shrub is commonly plant-ed for its golden yellow flowers in early spring. Although it blooms approximately at the same time as spicebush there can be no confusion between these two species since the flowers of forsythia are more showy and ornamental.

Shadbush/Serviceberry, *Amelanchier sp.*
Rose Family

Two species of shadbush are commonly found growing along the Palisades —Allegheny or smooth serviceberry, *A. laevis,* and downy serviceberry, *A. arborea.* It can be difficult to distinguish between the species. Both produce a fragile white flower in mid-April, the same time the fish known as shad return to spawn in the Hudson River. A small, apple-like fruit ripens in June, a critical food for wildlife when little else is available.

Red-Berried Elder, *Sambucus racemosa*
Honeysuckle Family

The small white flowers of this shrub are clustered in a cone-shaped arrangement, blooming by mid-April. The fruits ripen by mid-June and are readi-ly consumed by several species of birds. This shrub prefers to grow on rocky hillsides typical of the Palisades.

Flowering Dogwood, *Cornus florida*
Dogwood Family

Once a common understory tree of the northeastern woodland, many flowering dogwoods have succumbed to a deadly fungal disease. Flowering in May, some trees have survived, growing in more open, sunny areas. The bright red fruit is an important fall food for migratory and resident birds.

Black Haw, *Viburnum prunifolium*
Honeysuckle Family

A common shrub of the Palisades, clusters of small, white flowers bloom in early May. A dark blue-black fruit ripens by late summer, providing food for local wildlife. Note the warty, alligator bark of older specimens and an acrid smell after a heavy rain. This shrub prefers to grow along the ridge top near the cliff.

Maple-Leaved Viburnum, *Viburnum acerifolium*
Honeysuckle Family

Blooming from mid to late May, the flower shape is similar to the previous viburnum. This shrub prefers the shade, forming a dense understory in the mixed oak woodland. A dry, black fruit is produced in the fall and lingers well into November.

Deutzia*, *Deutzia scabra*
Hydrangea Family

This shrub, an escapee from cultivation, produces showy white blooms in June. A native of Japan and China, it was planted as an ornamental in gardens and parks. The fruit is a dry, brown capsule.

Mock Orange*, *Philadelphus coronarius*
Hydrangea Family
The white flowers of this shrub bloom from mid-May to early June and have a sweet fragrance resembling that of orange blossoms. A native of Southeastern Europe and Asia Minor, this species was once a popular plant of parks and gardens.

Black Raspberry, *Rubus occidentalis*
Rose Family
The small white flowers of this native raspberry produce a dark, purple berry that is one of our tastiest wild fruits. The whitish bloom on the purple stem is helpful in identifying this plant, which frequently grows in open areas where trees have fallen.

Wineberry*, *Rubus phoenicolasius*
Rose Family
Originally from eastern Asia, this plant has escaped cultivation, competing with our native plants. A small white flower ripens into a red, edible berry in July, a popular trailside nibble for hikers. The hairy, red stem is heavily armed with thorns.

Sweet Pepperbush, *Clethra alnifolia*
Clethra Family
A common shrub of wetlands, the fragrant white flowers bloom in midsummer providing a good place to find a variety of butterflies. Fruits mature into small brown capsules that persist in winter.

Japanese Honeysuckle*, *Lonicera japonicum*
Honeysuckle Family

This aggressive vine can climb or trail, producing dense tangles. The extremely fragrant flowers are white and yellow in color. The fruit is a shiny blackberry which is consumed and spread by birds. A native plant of eastern Asia, it is now commonly found throughout our area.

Eastern Redbud, *Cercis canadensis*
Caesalpinia Family

A small native tree that produces magenta-pink blooms in early spring before the leaves emerge. Found growing along the rocky hillsides of the Palisades, it is uncommon.

Pinkster Azalea, *Rhododendron periclymenoides*
Heath Family

The flowers can vary in color from pale to bright pink, blooming in early May. The showy blossoms attract butterflies such as the tiger and spicebush swallowtails. This shrub can tolerate the dry, rocky soils of the Palisades.

Mountain Laurel, *Kalmia latifolia*
Rhododendron Family

The spectacular pale-pink blooms of this native shrub are among the most anticipated. Blooming from late May until early June, this shrub can be found growing along the hillsides of the Palisades. The waxy leaves are evergreen and easily located in the winter.

Purple-Flowering Raspberry, *Rubus odoratus*
Rose Family

The deep pink flowers of this native raspberry are showy, blooming in June. This plant prefers the margins of woods, growing in partial shade. A fruit resembling a cultivated raspberry is formed by midsummer.

Allegheny-Vine/Climbing Fumitory,
Adlumia fungosa
Fumitory Family

This delicate vine can be found climbing on the talus slope. The distinctive heart-shaped flower is pale pink in color, blooming from mid to late summer. This is an endangered plant in New Jersey and can be difficult to locate when not in bloom.

False Indigo, *Amorpha fruticosa*
Pea/Bean Family

In June this shrub produces spikes of small purple blooms that are contrasted by bright orange anthers. Although this plant can survive in sterile soil, it prefers a moist habitat and can frequently be found growing along the Hudson River shoreline.

Wisteria*, *Wisteria floribunda*
Pea/Bean Family

A native plant of Japan, this high climbing vine has escaped cultivation. It produces extremely showy lavender flowers in mid-May that form bean-like pods in the fall. Mature vines can strangle their support trees.

Black Swallow-Wort*, *Vincetoxicum nigrum*
Milkweed Family

This vine is native to southern Europe and continues to invade the Palisades area. A difficult invasive to manage, this plant tends to smother native herbaceous plants by trailing over them. The small, black flowers produce pods with seeds that are readily dispersed on "parachutes," characteristic of this family.

Bladdernut, *Staphylea trifolia*
Bladderwort Family

The inflated seed pods are the most distinctive feature of this beautiful native shrub. The small bell-shaped white flowers are easily overlooked in late April to early May when they bloom. This shrub prefers the rocky hillsides of the talus slope and often grows in dense colonies.

Red-Berried Elder, *Sambucus racemosa*
Honeysuckle Family

The bright red berries of this shrub ripen mid to late June, providing an important food for birds. Note that the berries are toxic for human consumption.

Staghorn Sumac, *Rhus typhina*
Cashew Family

The large compound leaves, velvet covered stems and furry, red fruits help identify this plant. Preferring to grow in dry, sunny locations it can frequently be found growing along the cliff edge. The fruits are consumed by wildlife in late fall and through the winter.

Poison Ivy, *Toxicodendron radicans*
Cashew Family

This is one of the most common native plants of the Palisades community and a good one to learn in all growth forms. The three leaves are not always obvious in the field. Tiny white flowers are produced in late spring and followed by white fruits in the fall. The fruits are an important source of food for migrating and over-wintering birds. Note the hairy, reddish aerial roots produced by mature vines.

Wild Grape, *Vitis sp.*
Grape Family

Two species of wild grape are commonly found growing on the Palisades. Summer grape, *Vitis aestivalis,* prefers to grow in open thickets and along the roadside. Fox Grape, *Vitis labrusca,* can be found in shaded woods. Both species are ancestors of cultivated grapes, including the Concord. They produce a dark purple fruit in fall that is smaller in size but important for wildlife.

Virginia-creeper/Woodbine,
Parthenocissus quinquefolia
Grape Family

This high climbing vine has adhesive disks at the end of its tendrils, which can adhere to a variety of support surfaces including buildings, rocks and trees. The five-parted leaf turns a brilliant red in the fall and produces blue-black fruits that are consumed by wildlife.

Five-Leaf Akebia*,
Akebia quinata
Lardizabala Family

This high climbing, woody vine is a native of Eastern Asia and can grow to heights of 40 feet. The palmate leaf is tardily deciduous, holding onto its leaves well into the winter months. Escaped from cultivation, there is only one colony in the park at the Undercliff location.

White Oak, *Quercus alba*
Beech Family

A handsome tree of the upland woods, the distinctive flaky bark is pale gray in mature trees. A combination of successive droughts and gypsy moth infestations continue to threaten this species on the Palisades. The bright green acorns are readily collected and consumed by wildlife as soon as they ripen in late summer.

Chestnut Oak, *Quercus prinus*
Beech Family

The deeply furrowed bark helps to distinguish this oak. It can be found growing in upland, rocky woods and along the cliffs of the Palisades. The large acorns usually fall without their cap and quickly sprout a taproot, if they have not been collected by wildlife.

Black Oak, *Quercus velutina*
Beech Family

The dark, rough, pebbled bark is best distinguished in older specimens. Preferring to grow in dry, upland woods, this species survives well on the Palisades ridge. The smaller acorns, with caps covering half to three-quarters of the nut are often buried by wildlife to leach out the bitter tannic acids.

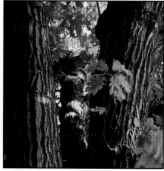

Northern Red Oak, *Quercus rubra*
Beech Family

The smooth gray bark with pale striations, give the tree a striped appearance. It prefers well-drained, acid soils of the upland woods. A thin cap covers only a small portion of the large acorn that is produced. This is the most common oak of the upland woods.

Black Birch, *Betula lenta*
Birch Family

The numerous horizontal striations known as lenticels are the easiest way to identify this tree. The bark is shiny, black in color, and the branches smell of wintergreen when broken. A common tree of the Palisades, it is sometimes found growing in rock crevices.

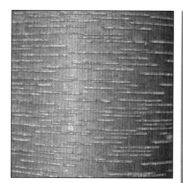

Paper Birch, *Betula papyrifera*
Birch Family

A rare tree in New Jersey, it is restricted to growing only on the talus slope, which provides cooler temperatures needed to survive. The white, peeling bark distinguishes this species from the more common gray birch, which can also be found on the Palisades.

American Sycamore, *Platanus occidentalis*
Plane-tree Family

This distinctive tree can often be found growing along river banks or in moist soil. As the tree matures, the peeling bark exposes a creamy white color underneath. Compare this species to the London Plane tree in the boat basin parking lot. It is a hybrid of the American and the Oriental sycamore, and as it exfoliates, it exposes a golden yellow bark.

Northern Hackberry, *Celtis occidentalis*
Elm Family

A small tree with bark that can appear warty as it matures. The asymmetrical leaves feel like sandpaper to the touch and a small, orange fruit is produced in the fall. This tree is the host plant for two species of butterflies in this area. Both the hackberry, and tawny emperor caterpillars feed exclusively on the leaves.

Eastern Hemlock, *Tsuga canadensis*
Pine Family

A tree of the northern woods, this evergreen prefers to grow in the cool ravines. Infected in the mid-1980's by a scale-like insect, wooley adelgid, most hemlocks on the Palisades died by the mid-1990's. The skeletal remains of these trees continue to be excavated primarily by woodpeckers. Occasionally a few young trees can be found in the park.

Austrian Pine*, *Pinus nigra*
Pine Family

A native tree of Europe, this species is often planted as a windbreak or screen and can adapt to a variety of soil conditions. The distinctively furrowed bark is best appreciated in mature specimens. The stiff, paired needles have a sharp point to the touch.

White Pine, *Pinus strobilus*
Pine Family

The soft, feathery needles are bundled in groups of five. With the loss of the Eastern hemlock, this has become an important tree, especially for roosting owls, that must sequester themselves during the day. This tree can be found growing in a variety of habitats throughout the Palisades.

Royal Paulownia*, *Paulownia tomentosa*
Trumpet-creeper Family

Native to China, it is also known as the Empress tree or Princess tree. The showy, purple flowers are very fragrant, blooming in mid-May. Young trees produce enormous leaves that are often a source of curiosity for park visitors. This tree may have escaped cultivation from the former estates that were once found along the Palisades.

Tulip Tree, *Liriodendron tulipifera*
Magnolia Family

This tree can be recognized by its very straight, limbless trunk that leafs out high in the canopy. It has showy, yellow-green flowers with orange interiors, which largely go unnoticed until they fall to the ground. The cone-like fruits mature in the fall, providing winter food for wildlife.

Tree-of-Heaven*, *Ailanthus altissima*
Quassia Family

The large compound leaf is sometimes mistaken for sumac. At the base of each ailanthus leaflet is a gland that produces a foul smell when crushed, accounting for the tree's alternate name, which is stinkweed. A native of eastern Asia, this tree is rapidly displacing our native plants. It produces a winged seed which turns a colorful red in fall. The success of this alien species is dependent on its adaptable nature, high tolerance to pollution and large number of seeds produced.

Spring Beauty, *Claytonia virginica*
Purslane Family

As the common name suggests, this plant blooms in early spring, preferring rich woods and woodland edges. If you look closely, the small, pale flower is highlighted with dark pink stripes. When found, this plant can blanket an area.

Wild Pink, *Silene caroliniana*
Pink Family

This brightly colored flower appears more horticultural than wild. It can be found growing in some of the most extreme habitats such as the crevices of the Palisades rock face and cliff edge. Considered rare in New Jersey, this plant blooms early to mid-May.

Herb-Robert*, *Geranium robertianum*
Geranium Family

The rose-colored bloom of this annual/biennial plant can be found growing along the edge of the moist, rocky woodlands of the Palisades. It can bloom from May until November, depending on the weather conditions. This plant is originally from Eurasia and is considered naturalized in our area.

Wild Geranium, *Geranium maculatum*
Geranium Family

These flowers, in various shades of pink, are similar in shape to the previous species but larger. This is a common spring wildflower of the Palisades woodlands, blooming from late April into early May.

Wild Columbine, *Aquilegia canadensis*
Buttercup Family

The showy red and yellow flowers of this spring wildflower prefer the dry woods and rocky cliff edges of the Palisades. Late April to early May is a good time to search for the blooms.

Dame's Rocket*, *Hesperis matronalis*
Mustard Family

This plant is considered an old-fashioned ornamental, that blooms in a variety of colors including purple, pink, and white. Originally from Eurasia, it escaped cultivation and now grows along roadsides and in open woods. Look for the flowers from early to mid-May.

Pasture Rose, *Rosa carolina*
Rose Family

This native rose blooms in June along the rocky cliff edges and open dry woods. The stems have few thorns which are slender and straight. The flowers range in color from dark pink to white, producing rose hips in late summer that persist into the winter.

Common Milkweed, *Asclepias syriaca*
Milkweed Family

The familiar brownish-pink blooms of this common wildflower are produced in early summer. Frequently found growing along the roadside, it can also be found in sunny fields and meadows. An important host plant of the monarch butterfly, this plant supports a wide variety of insects.

Sweet-Scented Joe-Pye Weed,
Eupatorium purpureum
Aster Family

This plant blooms in August and prefers to grow along dry, open woodland borders. There are several species of Joe-pye weed that grow on the Palisades, but this is the only one with a pale stem and deep purple joints on the main stalk of the plant.

Trout Lily, *Erythronium americanum*
Lily Family

This is an early spring wildflower that prefers to grow in moist woodlands. The leaves are distinctively mottled and can blanket the forest floor. Only a few plants produce the nodding, yellow flower each year.

Yellow Forest Violet, *Viola pubescens*
Violet Family

This early spring wildflower is uncommon to the Palisades, and grows trailside in moist woodlands. The pale, yellow flower is short lived, and blooms by late April. This violet belongs to the group that has leaves along the stem.

Perfoliate Bellwort, *Uvularia perfoliata*
Lily Family

The nodding, bell-shaped flower can be easily overlooked. Look for the distinctive leaf arrangement in which the stem seemingly pierces the leaves. A closer inspection of the flower will reveal the orange projections found inside, which bloom in late April to early May.

Jewelweed, *Impatiens capensis*
Touch-me-not Family

A wildflower commonly found growing along streams and moist woodlands. The orange flowers have reddish brown spots, blooming from mid summer to early fall, attracting many pollinators including ruby-throated hummingbirds.

Pale Jewelweed, *Impatiens pallida*
Touch-me-not Family

Similar to the previous species, the flowers are pale yellow in color, less spotted, and bloom from early to midsummer. This plant prefers to grow on the rocky, talus slope and along the shore trail.

Seaside Goldenrod, *Solidago sempervirens*
Aster Family

The presence of this wildflower along the shoreline confirms the salt marsh habitat of the Hudson River. This is a tall plant that can grow up to eight feet, with fleshy leaves that help to conserve water. A plume of yellow, star-shaped flowers blooms in late summer to early fall. This is an important food source for monarch butterflies migrating in the fall.

Blue-Stemmed Goldenrod, *Solidago caesia*
Aster Family

This late blooming flower prefers to grow along shaded woodland edges. The flowers are located in the leaf axils along the stem. Although it can be difficult to distinguish between goldenrod species, the two presented in this booklet are distinctively different.

Woodland Sunflower, *Helianthus divaricatus*
Aster Family

This native sunflower blooms from mid to late August, preferring open, dry woods and cliff edge habitat. It can reach six feet in height with sharply pointed leaves that have a rough upper surface. The oily seeds are a favorite food for some songbirds, especially goldfinch.

Day Lily*, *Hemerocallis fulva*
Lily Family

A cultivated plant that escaped from gardens of former estates on the Palisades. Where established, this plant can blanket an area, excluding other kinds of herbaceous plants. The showy, orange flower blooms around the summer solstice, producing a new flower each day until early July.

Lyre-leaved Rock Cress, *Arabis lyrata*
Mustard Family

One of our earliest spring wildflowers to bloom in April. It prefers the rock ledges and crevices of the Palisades. The white flowers are very small, but extremely fragrant and attract numerous early pollinators. The basal leaves are deeply lobed and form a rosette.

Early Saxifrage, *Saxifraga virginiensis*
Saxifrage Family

Another early spring wildflower that blooms in April along rocky trails and more sheltered rocky embankments. The stem is extremely hairy with small white flowers blooming in a branched cluster. A small basal rosette of leaves can usually be found growing in the crevice of a rock.

Dutchman's Breeches, *Dicentra cucullaria*
Fumitory Family

This is an early wildflower of the rocky hillsides. Fern-like foliage appears from mid to late April, producing a pantaloon-shaped flower that is suspended along the stem. Once pollinated, this plant quickly produces fruits that ripen into a distinctive green pod.

Garlic Mustard*, *Alliaria petiolata*
Mustard Family

A common invasive plant of the woodland, producing small white flowers in early spring and prolific quantities of seed by early summer. When crushed, the leaves have a strong odor. Originally from Eurasia, this plant produces dense colonies, crowding out native species.

Japanese Knotweed*, *Polygonum cuspidatum*
Buckwheat Family

Also known as Mexican bamboo, this plant escaped cultivation. A native of Japan, it has become well established in this area, growing along trails and roadside. The bamboo-like stalks are distinctly jointed and can reach heights of six to seven feet. By late August and early September, it produces an abundance of tiny, white flowers that ripen into a three-parted fruit.

White Wood Aster, *Aster divaricatus*
Aster Family

This is a common aster of the upland woods. The star-shaped white flowers bloom from late August into September, forming seeds that provide local birds and late migrants with important wildlife food.

Early Meadow Rue, *Thalictrum dioicum*
Buttercup Family

This wildflower blooms from mid to late April with male and female structures on separate plants. The male plant is showier, with yellow, pollen-filled tassels, often observed waving in the wind. The delicate leaflets appear at the same time as the flower, and are usually found growing along the rocky woodland slopes.

Wild Ginger, *Asarum canadense*
Birthwort Family

This wildflower is very rare on the Palisades. Once you have located the plant, you must get on your hands and knees to find the flower. Blooming in early spring, the reddish-brown flower grows close to the ground. The root was once used as a substitute for the commercial spice ginger.

Jack-in-the-Pulpit, *Arisaema triphyllum*
Arum Family

This unusual plant blooms by early May and produces bright, red fruits in the fall. The hooded leafy structure sometimes obscures the plant. The botanical term for the hood is the spathe, a structure that conceals the reproductive parts of the plant known as the spadix.

Mexican Tea*, *Chenopodium ambrosioides*
Goosefoot Family

This inconspicuous plant is best identified by crushing the leaves, which produce a pungent, medicinal odor. The flowers are small, green and almost indistinguishable from the foliage. An annual from tropical America, it can be found growing along disturbed portions of the Shore trail.

Periwinkle, Myrtle* *Vinca minor*
Dogbane Family

Once a plant of the garden, it has escaped cultivation and is invading parts of the woodland.
Blooming in early April, the bluish-purple flowers
often blanket an area. It's originally from southern
Europe.

Common Blue Violet, Dooryard Violet,
Viola sororia
Violet Family

One of our most familiar wildflowers, the basal
rosette of leaves produce a violet-colored flower.
Closer inspection will reveal a white beard inside
the throat of the flower. These wildflowers are
common trailside, growing in moist as well as
rocky habitats. The flowers persist from early to
mid spring.

Purple Loosestrife*, *Lythrum salicaria*
Loosestrife Family

The brilliant, magenta flowers are easy to recog-
nize and can be found blooming from late July into
early September, reaching heights of up to six feet.
A native of Eurasia, this plant can be very invasive,
preferring wetland habitats.

Asiatic Day Flower*, *Commelina communis*
Spiderwort Family

The blue petals of this interesting flower stand out
among the late summer and early fall greenery.
Two larger petals dwarf a reduced third petal that
requires close inspection to find. A native of eastern Asia, this plant prefers shaded woodland
edges and is not considered an invasive species.

FERNS

Marginal Shield Fern, *Dryopteris marginalis*
Spleenwort Family

This evergreen fern persists throughout the winter and can be found growing primarily on the talus slope and rocky woodland. The sporangia contain the spores or reproductive structures, and are found on the undersurface of the frond along the margins.

Christmas Fern, *Polystichum acrostichoides*
Spleenwort Family

This evergreen fern can be found throughout the year along woodland trails. The dark, shiny fronds are distinctively lobed at the base. The sporangia contain the spores or reproductive structures, and are found only on the upper portion of the fertile frond.

New York Fern, *Thelypteris noveboracensis*
Spleenwort Family

This is a small, delicate, deciduous fern that is found in open woods and along moist woodland edges. Characteristically tapering at both ends, it can cover extensive portions of the understory under optimal growing conditions.

Common Polypody, Rockcap Polypody
Polypodium virginianum
Polypody Family

This fern is usually found growing on the tops of boulders and on the talus slope. Note the large, bright orange sporangia on the undersurface of the frond.

Appendix A
Amphibians & Reptiles New Jersey Section

Amphibians:

Spotted Salamander *(Ambystoma maculatum)*

Northern Two-lined Salamander *(Eurycea bislineata)*

Northern Redback Salamander *(Plethodon cinereus)*

Northern Slimy Salamander *(Plethodon glutinosus)*

Northern Red Salamander *(Pseudotriton r. ruber)*

American Toad *(Bufo americanus)*

Northern Spring Peeper *(Pseudacris c. crucifer)*

Bullfrog *(Rana catesbeiana)*

Green Frog *(Rana clamitans melanota)*

Pickerel Frog *(Rana palustris)*

Wood Frog *(Rana sylvatica)*

Reptiles:

Common Snapping Turtle *(Chelydra s. serpentina)*

Eastern Painted Turtle *(Chrysemys p. picta)*

Wood Turtle *(Clemmys insculpta)*

Common Musk Turtle *(Sternotherus odoratus)*

Eastern Box Turtle *(Terrapene c. carolina)*

Five-lined Skink *(Eumeces fasciatus)*

Northern Copperhead Snake *(Agkistrodon contortrix mokasen)*

Northern Ringneck Snake *(Diadophis punctatus edwardsii)*

Black Rat Snake *(Elaphe o. obsoleta)*

Eastern Milk Snake *(Lampropeltis t. triangulum)*

Northern Water Snake *(Nerodia s. sipedon)*

Eastern Garter Snake *(Thamnophis s. sirtalis)*

Appendix B
Butterflies in New Jersey Section

Pipevine Swallowtail *(Battus philenor)*

Black Swallowtail *(Papilio polyxenes)*

Eastern Tiger Swallowtail *(Papilio glaucus)*

Spicebush Swallowtail *(Papilio troilus)*

Cabbage White *(Pieris rapae)*

Clouded Sulphur *(Colias philodice)*

Orange Sulphur *(Colias eurytheme)*

Cloudless Sulphur *(Phoebis sennae)*

American Copper *(Lycaena phlaeas)*

Banded Hairstreak *(Satyrium calanus)*

Hickory Hairstreak *(Satyrium caryaevorum)*

Striped Hairstreak *(Satyrium liparops)*

White M Hairstreak *(Parrhasius m-album)*

Gray Hairstreak *(Strymon melinus)*

Red-banded Hairstreak *(Calycopis cecrops)*

Eastern Tailed Blue *(Everes comyntas)*

Spring Azure *(Celastrina ladon)*

Great Spangled Fritillary *(Speyeria cybele)*

Silvery Checkerspot *(Chlosyne nycteis)*

Pearl Crescent *(Phyciodes tharos)*

Question Mark *(Polygonia interrogationis)*

Eastern Comma *(Polygonia comma)*

Compton Tortoiseshell *(Nymphalis vau-album)*

Mourning Cloak *(Nymphalis antiopa)*

American Lady *(Vanessa virginiensis)*

Painted Lady *(Vanessa cardui)*

Red Admiral *(Vanessa atalanta)*

Common Buckeye *(Junoinia coenia)*

Red-spotted Purple *(Limenitis arthemis astyanax)*

Hackberry Emperor *(Asterocampa celtis)*

Tawny Emperor *(Asterocampa clyton)*

Northern Pearly Eye *(Enodia anthedon)*

Little Wood Satyr *(Megisto cymela)*

Common Wood Nymph *(Cercyonis pegala)*

Monarch *(Danaus plexippus)*

Silver-spotted Skipper *(Epargyreus clarus)*

Hoary Edge *(Achalarus lyciades)*

Dreamy Duskywing *(Erynnis icelus)*

Juvenal's Duskywing *(Erynnis juvenalis)*

Wild Indigo Duskywing *(Erynnis baptisiae)*

Common Sootywing *(Pholisora catullus)*

Least Skipper *(Ancyloxypha numitor)*

Peck's Skipper *(Polites peckius)*

Northern Broken Dash *(Wallengrenia egeremet)*

Little Glassywing *(Pompeius verna)*

Mulberry Wing *(Poanes massasoit)*

Hobomok Skipper *(Poanes hobomok)*

Zabulon Skipper *(Poanes zabulon)*

Broad-winged Skipper *(Poanes viator)*

Dun Skipper *(Euphyes vestries)*

APPENDIX C
MAMMALS IN NEW JERSEY SECTION

Opossum *(Didelphis virginiana)*

Masked Shrew *(Sorex cinereus)*

Northern Short-tailed Shrew *(Blarina brevicauda)*

Star-nosed Mole *(Condylura cristata)*

Common Eastern Mole *(Scalopus aquaticus)*

Eastern Red Bat *(Lasiurus borealis)*

Eastern Pipistrelle *(Pipistrellus subflavus)*

Little Brown Bat *(Myotis lucifugus)*

Big Brown Bat *(Eptesicus fuscus)*

Eastern Cottontail *(Sylvilagus floridanus)*

Woodchuck *(Marmota monax)*

Eastern Chipmunk *(Tamias striatus)*

Eastern Gray Squirrel *(Sciurus carolinensis)*

Red Squirrel *(Tamiasciurus hudsonicus)*

Southern Flying Squirrel *(Glaucomys volans)*

White-footed Mouse *(Peromyscus leucopus)*

Meadow Vole *(Microtus pennsylvanicus)*

Woodland Vole *(Microtus pinetoreum)*

Muskrat *(Ondatra zibethicus)*

Allegheny Woodrat *(Neotoma magister)*

Norway Rat *(Rattus norvegicus)*

Red Fox *(Vulpes vulpes)*

Gray Fox *(Urocyon cinereoargenteus)*

Eastern Coyote *(Canis latrans)*

Raccoon *(Procyon lotor)*

Striped Skunk *(Mephitis mephitis)*

Long-tailed Weasel *(Mustela frenata)*

Black Bear *(Ursa americanus)*

White-tailed Deer *(Odocoileus virginianus)*

Appendix D
Birds in the New Jersey Section

Red-throated Loon M/W

Common Loon M

Pied-billed Grebe M

Horned Grebe M

Double-crested Cormorant M/S

American Bittern M/S

Least Bittern M

M	Migration (Spring and/or Fall)
W	Winter (December-February)
S	Summer (June-August)
Y	Year Round
*	Breeding

Great Blue Heron Y

Great Egret M/S

Snowy Egret M/S

Little Blue Heron M/S

Green Heron Y*

Black-crowned Night Heron M/S

Yellow-crowned Night Heron M

Glossy Ibis M

Black Vulture M

Turkey Vulture Y*

Snow Goose M/W

Canada Goose Y*

Brant M/W

Mute Swan M/W

Tundra (Whistling) Swan M/W

Wood Duck Y*

Gadwall M/W

American Widgeon M

American Black Duck Y

Mallard Y*

Blue-winged Teal M

Northern Shoveler M

Northern Pintail M/W

Green-winged Teal M

Canvasback W

Redhead M

Ring-necked Duck M

Greater Scaup W

Lesser Scaup W

White-winged Scoter M/W

Black Scoter M/W

Bufflehead W

Common Goldeneye M/W

Hooded Merganser M

Common Merganser M/W

Red-breasted Merganser M/W

Ruddy Duck M/W

Osprey M/S

Bald Eagle Y

Northern Harrier M/W

Sharp-shinned Hawk M/W

Cooper's Hawk Y*

Northern Goshawk M/W

Red-shouldered Hawk Y

Broad-winged Hawk Y*

Red-tailed Hawk Y*

Rough-legged Hawk M/W

Golden Eagle M

American Kestrel Y

Merlin M/W

Peregrine Falcon Y*

Ring-necked Pheasant M/S

Ruffed Grouse Y*

Wild Turkey Y*

Common Moorhen M/S

American Coot M

Killdeer M/S

Greater Yellowlegs M

Lesser Yellowlegs M

Solitary Sandpiper M/S

Spotted Sandpiper M/S

Least Sandpiper M

Common Snipe M

American Woodcock M/W

Laughing Gull M/W

Bonaparte's Gull M/W

Ring-billed Gull Y

Herring Gull Y

Iceland Gull M/W

Glaucous Gull M/W

Great Black-backed Gull Y

Caspian Tern M

Common Tern M/S

Black Skimmer M

Rock Dove Y*

Mourning Dove Y*

Monk Parakeet Y

Black-billed Cuckoo M/S*

Yellow-billed Cuckoo M/S*

Eastern Screech Owl Y*

Great Horned Owl Y*

Long-eared Owl M/W

Short-eared Owl M

Northern Saw-whet Owl M/W

Common Nighthawk M/S

Whip-poor-will M

Chimney Swift M/S

Ruby-throated Hummingbird M/S*

Belted Kingfisher Y

Red-headed Woodpecker M/S

Red-bellied Woodpecker Y*

Yellow-bellied Sapsucker M/W

Downy Woodpecker Y*

Hairy Woodpecker Y*

Northern Flicker Y*

Pileated Woodpecker Y*

Olive-sided flycatcher M

Eastern Wood Pewee M/S*

Yellow-bellied Flycatcher M

Acadian Flycatcher M

Alder Flycatcher M

Willow Flycatcher M

Least Flycatcher M

Eastern Phoebe M/S*

Great Crested Flycatcher M/S*

Eastern Kingbird M/S*

White-eyed Vireo M

Yellow-throated Vireo M/S*

Blue-headed Vireo M

Warbling Vireo M/S*

Philadelphia Vireo M

Red-eyed Vireo M/S*

Blue Jay Y*

American Crow Y*

Fish Crow M/S

Common Raven Y*

Purple Martin M

Tree Swallow M/S

Northern Rough-winged Swallow M/S*

Bank Swallow M

Cliff Swallow M

Barn Swallow M/S*

Black-capped Chickadee Y*

Boreal Chickadee W

Tufted Titmouse Y*

Red-breasted Nuthatch Y

White-breasted Nuthatch Y*

Brown Creeper M/W

Carolina Wren Y*

House Wren M/S*

Winter Wren Y*

Sedge Wren M

Marsh Wren M

Golden-crowned Kinglet M/W

Ruby-crowned Kinglet M/W

Blue-gray Gnatcatcher M/S*

Eastern Bluebird M

Veery M/S*

Gray-cheeked Thrush M

Swainson's Thrush M

Hermit Thrush M/W

Wood Thrush Y*

American Robin Y*

Gray Catbird Y*

Northern Mockingbird Y*

Brown Thrasher Y*

European Starling Y*

Cedar Waxwing Y*

Blue-winged Warbler M/S*

Golden-winged Warbler M

Brewster's Warbler M

Lawrence's Warbler M

Tennessee Warbler M

Orange-crowned Warbler M

Nashville Warbler M

Northern Parula Warbler M

Yellow Warbler M/S*

Chestnut-sided Warbler M

Magnolia Warbler M

Cape May Warbler M

Black-throated Blue Warbler M

Yellow-rumped Warbler M/W

Black-throated Green Warbler M

Blackburnian Warbler M

Yellow-throated Warbler M

Pine Warbler M/W

Prairie Warbler M

Palm Warbler M

Bay-breasted Warbler M

Blackpoll Warbler M

Cerulean Warbler M

Black and White Warbler M/S*

American Redstart M/S*

Prothonotary Warbler M

Worm-eating Warbler M/S*

Ovenbird M/S*

Northern Waterthrush M/S

Louisiana Waterthrush M/S*

Kentucky Warbler M

Connecticut Warbler M

Mourning Warbler M

Common Yellowthroat M/S*

Hooded Warbler M/S*

Wilson's Warbler M

Canada Warbler M/S

Yellow-breasted Chat M

Summer Tanager M

Scarlet Tanager M/S*

Eastern Towhee Y*

American Tree Sparrow M/W

Chipping Sparrow Y*

Field Sparrow M/W

Vesper Sparrow M

Savannah Sparrow M

Fox Sparrow M/W

Song Sparrow Y*

Lincoln's Sparrow M

Swamp Sparrow M/W

White-throated Sparrow M/W

White-crowned Sparrow M

Dark-eyed Junco M/W

Snow Bunting M/W

Northern Cardinal Y*

Rose-breasted Grosbeak M/S*

Blue Grosbeak M/S*

Indigo Bunting M/S*

Dickcissel M

Bobolink M

Red-winged Blackbird Y*

Eastern Meadowlark M

Rusty Blackbird M

Common Grackle Y*

Brown-headed Cowbird Y*

Orchard Oriole M/S*

Baltimore Oriole M/S*

Pine Grosbeak W

Purple Finch M/W

House Finch Y*

Red Crossbill W

White-winged Crossbill W

Common Redpoll W

Pine Siskin M/W

American Goldfinch Y*

Evening Grosbeak M/W

House Sparrow Y*

Appendix E
Trees, Shrubs, and Vines

Allegheny-vine *(Adlumia fungosa)*

Alternate-leaved Dogwood *(Cornus alternifolia)*

American Sycamore *(Platanus occidentalis)*

Appalachian Gooseberry *(Ribes rotundifolium)*

Asiatic Bittersweet *(Celastrus orbiculatus)*

Austrian Pine *(Pinus nigra)*

Black Birch *(Betula lenta)*

Black Haw *(Viburnum prunifolium)*

Black Huckleberry *(Gaylussacia baccata)*

Black Oak *(Quercus velutina)*

Black Sour Gum *(Nyssa sylvatica)*

Black Swallow-wort *(Vincetoxicum nigrum)*

Black Walnut *(Juglans nigra)*

Black Raspberry *(Rubus occidentalis)*

Bladdernut *(Staphylea trifolia)*

Chestnut Oak *(Quercus prinus)*

Deutzia *(Deutzia scabra)*

Dogwood *(Cornus florida)*

Dutchman's Pipe *(Aristolochia macrophylla)*

Eastern Hemlock *(Tsuga canadensis)*

Eastern Red Cedar *(Juniperus virginiana)*

Eastern Redbud *(Cercis canadensis)*

False Indigo *(Amorpha fruticosa)*

Five-leaved Akebia *(Akibia quinata)*

Forsythia *(Forsythia x intermedia)*

Fox Grape *(Vitis labrusca)*

Groundsel-tree *(Baccharis halimifolia)*

Hackberry *(Celtis occidentalis)*

Highbush Blueberry *(Vaccinium corymbosum)*

Hillside Blueberry *(Vaccinium pallidum)*

Japanese Honeysuckle *(Lonicera japonicum)*

Maple-leaved Viburnum *(Viburnum acerifolium)*

Mock Orange *(Philadelphus coronarius)*

Mockernut Hickory *(Carya tomentosa)*

Mountain Laurel *(Kalmia latifolia)*

Multiflora Rose *(Rosa multiflora)*

Northern Red Oak *(Quercus rubra)*

Paper Birch *(Betula papyrifera)*

Pignut Hickory *(Carya glabra)*

Pinkster Azalea *(Rhododendron periclymenoides)*

Poison Ivy *(Toxicodendron radicans)*

Purple-flowering Raspberry *(Rubus odoratus)*

Red-berried Elder *(Sambucus racemosa)*

Round-leaved Dogwood *(Cornus rugosa)*

Royal Paulownia *(Paulownia tomentosa)*

Shadbush *(Amelenchier arborea)*

Shadbush *(Amelenchier laevis)*

Spicebush *(Lindera benzoin)*

Staghorn Sumac *(Rhus typhina)*

Summer Grape *(Vitis aestivalis)*

Swamp White Oak *(Quercus bicolor)*

Sweet Gum *(Liquidambar styraciflua)*

Sweet Pepperbush *(Clethra alnifolia)*

Tree-of-heaven *(Ailanthus altissima)*

Tulip Tree *(Liriodendron tulipifera)*

Virginia Creeper/Woodbine *(Parthenocissus quinquefolia)*

White Oak *(Quercus alba)*

White Pine *(Pinus strobilus)*

Wineberry *(Rubus phoenicolasius)*

Wisteria *(Wisteria floribunda)*

APPENDIX F
WILDFLOWERS, FERNS, AND GRASSES

Arrow-leaved Violet *(Viola sagittata)*

Asiatic Day Flower *(Commelina communis)*

Bitter Dock *(Rumex obtusifolius)*

Blue-stemmed Goldenrod *(Solidago caesia)*

Christmas Fern *(Polystichum acrostichoides)*

Common Polypody *(Polypodium virginianum)*

Common Blue Violet *(Viola sororia)*

Common Milkweed *(Asclepias syriaca)*

Dame's Rocket *(Hesperis matronalis)*

Day Lily *(Hemerocallis fulva)*

Dutchman's Breeches *(Dicentra cucullaria)*

Early Meadow Rue *(Thalictrum dioicum)*

Early Saxifrage *(Saxifraga virginiensis)*

False Solomon's Seal *(Smilacina racemosa)*

Garlic Mustard *(Alliaria petiolata)*

Hairy Solomon's Seal *(Polygonatum pubescens)*

Herb-Robert *(Geranium robertianum)*

Jack-in-the-pulpit *(Arisaema triphyllum)*

Japanese Knotweed *(Polygonum cuspidatum)*

Jewelweed *(Impatiens capensis)*

Lyre-leaved Rock Cress *(Arabis lyrata)*

Marginal Shield Fern *(Dryopteris marginalis)*

Mexican Tea *(Chenopodium ambrosioides)*

New York Fern *(Thelypteris noveboracensis)*

One-flowered Cancer-root *(Orobanche uniflora)*

Pale Jewelweed *(Impatiens pallida)*

Partridgeberry *(Mitchella repens)*

Pasture Rose *(Rosa carolina)*

Perfoliate Bellwort *(Uvularia perfoliata)*

Periwinkle/Myrtle *(Vinca minor)*

Phragmites/Common Reed *(Phragmites australis)*

Porcelain-berry *(Ampelopsis brevipedunculata)*

Purple Loosestrife *(Lythrum salicaria)*

Round-leaved Hepatica *(Hepatica americana)*

Round-leaved Pyrola *(Pyrola rotundifolia)*

Salt Marsh Cord Grass *(Spartina alterniflora)*

Salt Meadow Cord Grass *(Spartina patens)*

Seaside Goldenrod *(Solidago sempervirens)*

Skunk Cabbage *(Symplocarpus foetidus)*

Spearscale *(Atriplex patula)*

Spring Beauty *(Claytonia virginica)*

Sweet-scented Joe-pye-weed *(Eupatorium purpureum)*

Trout Lily *(Erythronium americanum)*

White Wood Aster *(Aster divaricatus)*

Wild Columbine *(Aquilegia canadensis)*

Wild Geranium *(Geranium maculatum)*

Wild Ginger *(Asarum canadense)*

Wild Pink *(Silene caroliniana)*

Wild Sarsparilla *(Aralia nudicaulis)*

Woodland Sunflower *(Helianthus divaricatus)*

Yellow Forest Violet *(Viola pubescens)*

INDEX

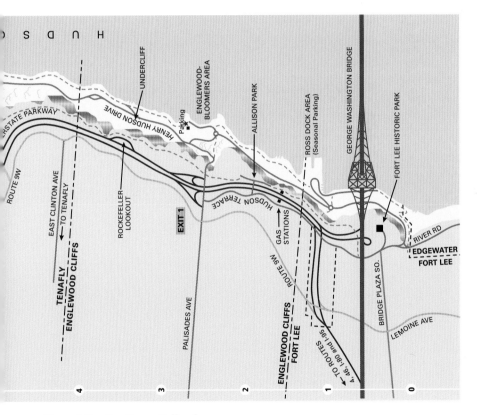

Map of the Southern Palisades

*This map includes all five hikes listed in the trail guide, from the
Englewood Boat Basin to Tallman State Park. Hike 4 identifies the
connecting trail between the Long Path, located at the top of the
Palisades, and the Shore Trail located along the Hudson River.*

A red star identifies the start of each hike.
  Hike 1 Undercliff Trail
  Hike 2 Alpine Long Path
  Hike 3 Alpine Shore Trail
  Hike 4 Forest View Trail
  Hike 5 Tallman Trail